D1496606

# Kopotuk, the Eskimo
## and Other Stories

*Willy Lou Warbelow*

# Kopotuk, the Eskimo
## and Other Stories

### Willy Lou Warbelow
Michael C. Anderson, Illustrator

Willy Lou Warbelow
Tok, Alaska

Published 1987

| First Printing | May 1987 |
| Second Printing | October 1989 |
| Third Printing | August 1993 |
| Fourth Printing | September 1997 |

ISBN No. 0-9618314-0-5

MAIN STREET ALASKA
PUBLISHING COMPANY
Box 252
Tok, Alaska 99780

## Dedication

To all our grandchildren who listen so willingly to my stories.

# Contents

Other books by the author

HEAD WINDS
EMPIRE ON ICE
CHILD OF THE EQUINOX
THE GUFFINY'S CHIMNEY

# FOREWORD

Willy Lou and Marvin Warbelow came to Alaska from Wisconsin as newlyweds in 1945. For eleven years they taught school with the Bureau of Indian Affairs in Eskimo villages of the Arctic and an Indian village in Interior Alaska.

From 1956 until 1970, with their daughter and three sons, they owned and operated their own lodge and air taxi service on the Alaska Highway. After her husband's death, Mrs. Warbelow transferred the air service to her sons, and she still works in the business with them. Her story of Marvin's 22 years of flying in Alaska, HEAD WINDS, was published during the summer of 1987.

Willy Lou and her present husband, Dale Young, now live in Tok, Alaska. They have a second home on Big Island in Hawaii where they are developing a Kona coffee farm.

Mary I. Roberts

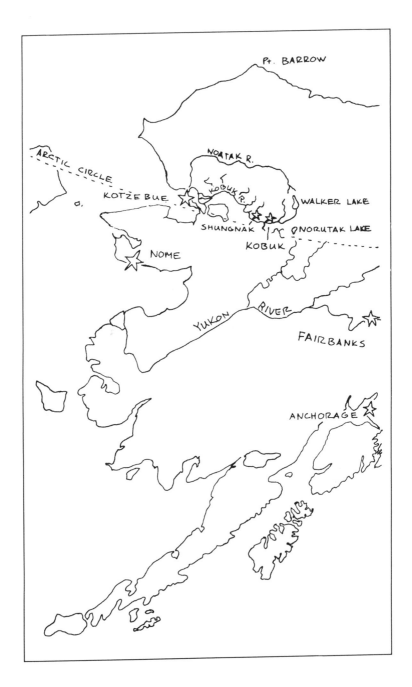

# PREFACE

During our three years in the small village of Shungnak on the Kobuk River Marvin and I learned as much from our Eskimo neighbors about their native skills and crafts, their happy dispositions, and their entire way of life as they learned from the pages of our school books. We worked side by side with them to establish their first native co-op store, to gain a post office for the village, and to stake claims on the jade deposits at the head of the Shungnak River.

This little book includes four chapters of a larger manuscript about our lives in the village. It brings out the fact that, in addition to all the activities within the village, there were many other things going on in the Arctic beyond the boundaries of Shungnak. I hope some day soon to publish my entire story.

Willy Lou Warbelow

# KOPOTUK

Kopotuk was one of the most fascinating persons we had ever known. When the missionaries came to the Arctic, they encouraged the native people to adopt white man type names for the sake of convenience, since in their own language each person had only one name. So names like Grey, Cleveland, Stringer, Black and Carlson appeared; and each person had a first and last name in addition to his own Eskimo name. Kopotuk became Charlie Coffin, but he was one of the few villagers we called by his native name.

He was the oldest man in the village. No more than five feet tall, he had a shock of snow white hair that set off his black eyes and the leatherness of his dark skin, and his expressive face. He walked with a kink in his back. One of the hardest workers in the village, he was always a bundle of enthusiasm, took his religion seriously and was a top-notch storyteller. English was difficult for him and he was continually groping for words to express himself, so any communication between us went at a snail's pace. He came up the hill often to visit and from him we learned some priceless Eskimo history.

He had been raised in Kalla, some distance up river. His childhood home was a true igloo made of chunks of sod much like the one igloo we had in Shungnak. In the center of the room, directly under the seal gut window, Kopotuk's father dug a hole in the dirt floor. This was the family's fire pit. Whenever a fire was burning, the window was opened to let the smoke out; but as soon as the fire died down, the window was sealed shut again. Eskimos then, and even in the forties when I knew them, weren't lavish with their heat. The purpose for building their home partially underground was to add warmth; and their fur clothing they wore constantly in cold weather served as an insulator so they could be comfortable in an unheated cabin. Wood was not only sometimes hard to come by, but their homemade tools made wood cutting a slow and difficult job. With proper foresight, the native people seldom cut wood near their homes, and this necessitated hauling fire logs sometimes long distances by dog sled. Or for those who didn't have dogs, it meant pulling the sled themselves.

"My papa make his own stove, too," Kopotuk told us. "He find big tree and cut off stump maybe like this." He extended his hands to indicate a length of about two feet. "He hollow out one end of stump with chisel and set it down on floor like bowl."

"Where did you get a chisel?" Marvin wanted to know.

"Oh-h-h, my papa make. He find long, sharp stone and some wood for handle. Then he tie stone to handle with rope he make from caribou leather.

2

"When my mama get ready to cook, she fill hollow stump maybe half full water. She make stones hot in fire pit and put in water. Then she put some kind meat. Stones make water hot and meat cook."

"What kind of meat did you have, Charlie?"

"Oh, we have caribou sometime or moose or bear. Maybe in sometime grayling or whitefish. My papa make big plate like this outta wood." His hands formed an imaginary dish. "When meat finish to cook, my mama put pieces on dish. We all sit on floor and eat."

"No forks?" I asked.

He smiled and shook his head. "No — no fork. We eat with finger. My papa even make cup with wood, too, and we drink broth from hot meat."

Then Kopotuk told us how he and a boy from a neighboring family roamed the woods all summer picking berries and slingshotting at a variety of little ground and tree animals, or lolled on the river banks fighting off hoards of mosquitoes with smudges.

"That must have been a happy way to live," I remarked. "No school to worry about — no taxes!"

Kopotuk suddenly sat up straighter in his chair, his eyes snapping, and he said emphatically, "No. No happy."

In his halting, limited English, he made us feel that life had been boring and monotonous, and he felt little purpose in living. It was a timeless thing with nothing but the seasons to break the monotony. Even the food, he said, offered no variety. The meat was saltless and, of course, the broth too. Beyond that they had not much more than berries and birds and the greens they pulled from the river bottom to cook in the wooden pot.

Each spring the family of Kopotuk loaded its meager belongings and caribou skins into the boat with the dogs and a supply of dried meat, and set off for the long trip down the Kobuk River to its mouth at the village of Kotzebue.

"It take us long time, that trip. We always drift, and if water go slow, we go slow. My papa have paddles and some other kind long poles we use when we get stuck on sand bars, and maybe if river carry us too close to bank, we can push off."

They passed by such spots as are now the villages of Kobuk and Shungnak, past the mouth of the beautiful Ambler River and on down to Kiana and Noorvik, across the big Kobuk Lake and finally to Kotzebue itself, the hub of the Arctic in that area.

"Every mans and families comes from every place all around to make summer in Kotzebue," he explained dramatically. "All the caribou peoples come from river villages like my own peoples come. From Noatak River and from Kobuk and any river. Then saltwater Eskimos come from islands and from up coast and down coast. We bring our caribou skins, and saltwater peoples have lotsa pokes fresh seal oil and big piles sealskin rope. We make lotsa trade these peoples."

It was a gala time when the boatloads of families, tents and dogs converged on the spit and began setting up temporary homes for the summer all along the shore and around the edges of the village. These summers were the happiest times of Kopotuk's young life, and he reminisced them tenderly. Each spring as old friends met, there was much shaking of hands, bouncing up and down and laughing, and dancing and singing among the elders before they settled down to the serious business of fishing for their winter's supply of food for themselves and the dogs.

While the grown-ups were renewing old acquaintances from previous years, the younger set was doing the same in a different fashion. Last year's playmates had grown a head taller and changed in appearance; the boys' voices that had been high pitched and childish just a few months before, were deeper and a little uncertain with a cracking now and then. So they felt shy with one another and each stayed close to his own tent until curiosity finally overcame the shyness, and little by little they began to mingle and exchange short greetings. Then finally came the long, endless days of constant companionship and running over the tundra for berries or playing in the icy lines of water that rolled onto the beach from the great ocean.

Here Kopotuk saw his first white man. The whaling ships were plying the waters between Seattle and Barrow in quest of the long strips of the fabulous black baleen from the mouths of giant whales that made their homes in the Arctic Ocean at the top of the world. On the way north the ships stopped off at Nome and Kotzebue to do a bit of business on the side. Kopotuk remembered the day a whaling boat docked off the coast, and smaller boats brought the sailors to shore.

"These white mans from boat all look us. I see one man come to me, and he have nice face to me, like smile. I see he have lo-o-ng beard, all white. Eskimo never see that kind before. He pat me on my head and say, 'My boy,' but I no call him Papa!"

He remembered, too, the first time he tasted salt, and the first match he struck. The salt came from the big ship. Probably his father had traded a few choice marten or mink skins for it and made it well worth the sailor's time to stay and barter. The matches that no doubt also came from the white man's ship were called Chinese matches. A whole box of matches had one solid head; and each match stick as it was broken from the mass, took a portion of the solid head with it — enough to spark a fire.

Summers in the Arctic are short and violent, and winters come early. As the days began to shorten and the nights to chill, the Eskimo families pulled in their nets and folded them away until the next spring. Dried fish was tied in bundles and stored in the big boats along with the tents and cooking gear and the dogs and ropes. The caribou skins had been replaced by pokes of oil and twists of sealskin rope that would make snowshoes and lashings for their sleds when winter came. Then with many goodbys, the families set off in their various directions for their winter homes.

The trip up river in the fall was a much slower and more difficult one than the ride down in the spring. It took the family six weeks to fight its way upstream by pushing with long poles against the river bottom near shore. Whenever the river bank was free of buckbrush, the men put some of the dogs ashore with long ropes tied to the boat and let them pull until the brush or willows crowded them out again. Snow usually found its way to their igloo at Kalla before the family did each fall, so the fire pit and the shelter of the four sod walls were a welcome sight. With salt to season their meat and Chinese matches to light their fire, life became just two steps more pleasant.

The Kopotuk we knew in the 1940s was all of seventy years old and just beginning to receive his monthly old age pension checks of twenty-five dollars. He was an independent old fellow who still set his fish net every summer and ran a short trapline during the winter. So with his monthly check to supplement his few needs, he did very nicely. His cabin was old and no longer to his liking, so during the summer of '46, he started his new house.

Every morning he trudged in his own stooped little way with his arms swinging back and forth away from his body out to the wood cutting area where he harvested his logs for the small cabin he would build. When that part of his work was done, he lashed them together into a raft, floated them down the river to the village, and one by one rolled them up the bank to his cabin site. Why he chose a spot so close to the river we could not understand; but with the high water at breakup time lapping away at his very doorstep, he had to build a retaining wall across the whole front side. For this he needed good sized boulders not to be found in the village, so up the hill he came one day to borrow the school wheelbarrow. He could haul only one rock at a time and the trip to his source of boulders was either a long one or a rough one, because we never saw him bring in more than three rocks a day even though he worked at it from morning until night.

The rocks were finally collected and cement mixed, and with help from just about no one, Kopotuk completed his rock wall. We couldn't help but wonder why the young fellows who strolled aimlessly or napped at midday in their bunks didn't offer a hand. But then we wondered the same thing in the dead of winter when the old women who lived in houses alone shuffled up river along the bank every day and returned hours later with bundles of willows to make small fires. They didn't get any offers of help either.

The wheelbarrow didn't come back to the school until the rock wall was finished. Marvin was perturbed when he noted that the whole front edge was badly battered. Kopotuk wasn't one you would want to offend, so Marvin delayed for some time before he finally found the opportunity to ask in a very polite manner just what had happened to the wheelbarrow.

The twinkly-eyed old Eskimo, proud of his carpentry and likewise his masonry, and always happy to talk about it, explained with enthusiasm, "I use that kind when I make my wall. When I put one rock and mortar, I can push

7

wheelbarrow up fast and give it big hit. That make it sit down tight on other rocks!"

"Kind of hard on my wheelbarrow, don't you think?" Marvin reproved him.

But Kopotuk chose that moment not to understand the English language and the matter was discussed no further.

Just as the sod igloo at Kalla had been built over a hole in the ground, so was the new log cabin at Shungnak sixty years later. We stooped when we went through the door and walked down two steps to the dirt floor. One small glass window looking over the river took the place of the sealgut skylight; and when all was finished, Kopotuk brought in armfuls of fresh spruce boughs to scatter over the floor for carpeting. Except for his homemade stove, there was no furniture in the cabin. He spread his furs on the floor for a bed, stirred up his sourdough hotcakes in a pan on the floor, and ate squatting down with his plate in front of him.

We were lavish in our praises of his new home as was the rest of the village and for a while after he moved, he had a surplus of visitors. But it wasn't long until he began to complain of arthritis and rheumatism and stiffnesses of all sorts. Marvin had to dig deep into the pill boxes and bottles in the school dispensary to keep him on his feet. Finally Marvin decided to have a talk with him.

"Kopotuk, you've had stiff joints ever since you moved into that new house. If you'd build yourself a low bunk, even a foot or so off the floor and get away from that dampness, I think you would feel better."

Kopotuk was indignant. "I never live in a house with bed and chair and table in my whole life!" he declared. "Too old to start now, I live on floor always. Floor is good for me now."

8

But then came the business of the bread baking and that's another story.

A few weeks after the move to the new cabin, Kopotuk called on us. We thought the visit came about because he had given himself a haircut and wanted to show it off. How he managed it we never found out, but it looked as though he had put his soup bowl on like a cap and cut around the edges. His white hair bounced out away from his head like an albino mushroom and he was proud of his handiwork.

But that wasn't the whole reason for his visit. Once the barbering had been discussed and was out of the way, he came right to the point.

"I eat bread your house some time when I come. Good bread. I think now new house — maybe I cook more. Maybe you teach me how you make bread?"

"Good idea, Charlie!" I agreed. "I think bread good for old man to eat. Keep you young."

"Then you teach me?" he asked eagerly.

"Sure I'll teach you. But I think maybe it's better if you come up to school tomorrow morning and watch the cook make a batch of bread for the school children. It might be easier for you to learn that way."

The next morning at eight o'clock sharp, Kopotuk was at the door for his bread-baking lesson. He didn't need as big a batch as the cook was making; so as she poured and added and mixed and kneaded, he was mentally dividing the ingredients by three and saying out loud, "Three for you, one for Charlie — six for you, two for Charlie." Then, with his recipe crammed into his head, he stopped by my kitchen on the way home.

"You come my house tomorrow when school finish. I have piece of bread for you!"

That afternoon he was back again to talk Marvin out of some choice pieces of packing boxes we had hoarded from

supplies that had come in the previous summer. Marvin didn't ask why he needed them, but I soon found out.

When I went down to the village the next day to collect my slice of bread, Kopotuk had three fresh loaves sitting on a wobbly-legged table made from the crating material and covered with a clean white flour sack that had been raveled and spread out flat for a tablecloth. You couldn't, he explained, put a batch of freshly baked homemade bread on the floor!

The bread baking created another problem. Like any cook with a new recipe, he was making bread about every other day for a while. But one day he came up to consult with us.

"When I make bread, it have three loaf, but I got only two tin." He held up three and then two fingers to emphasize his point. "So I always use tin from my neighbor. But when Eskimo borrow, he never take tin back empty, so I alla time have to give my neighbor one loaf bread. I think long time about that. Something not right for me. I make three loaf. I only get two loaf."

He had no solution to his problem but thought maybe we would. So after much thinking it over and exploring all possible avenues of escape, Marvin arrived at an excellent idea.

"Maybe we can teach you how to make a smaller batch of dough and you can get it all in your own two tins."

So for the rest of the winter, Kopotuk turned out a two-loaf batch of bread, kept one loaf to eat fresh, and carefully stashed the other loaf on top of his roof to freeze.

Although the table stayed in the house, the bunk-bed never materialized. Kopotuk slept on the floor, fought the rheumatism all winter, and when the rest of the village got hit with the flu, so did he. By the end of the second day we had almost no kids left in school. So we closed the classroom doors and Marvin made the rounds of the village every day with pockets full of pill bottles. Eskimos love to take pills, so he was a welcome visitor, and handfuls of pink and white and brown pills were left behind at every cabin. Every cabin, that is, except Kopotuk's. He had his own remedy for flu. He drank three fingers of seal oil from a gallon jug every morning and rubbed kerosene on his chest at night.

Almost any time of day during the cold winter months, we could see people going for firewood or bringing it home. The families with dog teams brought it in by the sledload. Those without dogs either pulled sleds by hand or hauled it on their shoulders or in their arms. Only once did we see anyone manage the firewood problem differently. The native lay reader and his family, temporary residents at Shungnak one year, came back down river from their fishing camp that summer with their sleds, dogs and household goods loaded on top of a huge raft they had built of freshly cut logs. Once the raft had served its purpose, they tore it apart and had their winter's wood supply.

Even Kopotuk, with all his foresight and ambition, never had more than a few days' supply in storage. So one cold day when he came in after dark with his three dogs pulling a sled-load of logs, Marvin asked him, "Why don't you plan ahead and have all this wood cut before winter sets in?"

With a look of tolerant patience, Kopotuk explained. "I try that once," he said. "All summer I cut and pile wood and have enough for whole winter. Then old lady get sick. She got no wood. I got wood, so I give her some. Then young girl have baby bad sick. She can't leave baby. She can't get wood. I have to give her wood. Then we have long cold many days. Many mans can't go for wood. Many houses cold. I still got wood. I give more wood to peoples. Pretty soon I got no wood too, so I never bring in plenty wood again, I go every day just like other peoples."

Once during a visit, Kopotuk made reference to his daughters. We both registered some surprise, I'm sure, because somehow we had never thought of our old friend as being a family man. It was many months later when we knew him much better, that he offered more information on his personal life. It seems that as a young man he had married and had two daughters. Then a white man coming into the area met his wife, and she eventually took the girls and went away with him. It must have been a blow to Kopotuk, because as he told the story his eyes filled with tears.

Some months later he received an official sounding letter from Nome saying that his wife was suing for divorce and the hearing would come before the court on a specified date the following mid-winter. Kopotuk assumed the letter was a summons for him to appear in court on that date. So that fall as soon as the rivers froze and winter set in, he harnessed his dogs, filled his sled with supplies, and started out on the long trip of several hundred miles to Nome. He had been to

Kotzebue many times, but knew nothing of the area between the Kobuk Valley and Nome on the underside of the Seward Peninsula. He followed his nose and the advice of the villagers he met along the way and arrived in Nome on schedule, only to discover that his presence hadn't even been requested. So he took on a new load of supplies, turned his team around and started the long lonesome trek back to the land that was home and that he knew. Early the next spring he finally mushed into Shungnak again.

When the girls grew up and married, they came back to Shungnak to visit their father, and although they never visited the years we lived there, they always kept in touch with him.

One morning during our last year in the village, Kopotuk came to the office to have me write a letter for him. I had written letters for him before, so I knew the procedure. I always sat at the typewriter and waited dutifully as he clasped his hands behind his back, looked down at the floor and paced thoughtfully back and forth while he dictated like an executive and I typed like a secretary. Then, because I was a terrible typist, I'd have to redo the whole letter, throw the original copy into the waste basket and submit the second one to him for his signature. But I wasn't expecting what he had in mind on this particular day when he came to see us.

He had just received word that his youngest daughter was in the Native Service hospital at Kotzebue dying of tuberculosis. He clasped his hands behind his back, lowered his head, began his slow pacing, and dictated the most eloquent message I have ever heard. It began, "My dear daughter Otha: The time has come for you to meet your Maker. I want you to go without fear, because you have led a good and Christian life."

What he said beyond that I don't recall, but the letter was short — just one page long — and it ended with the words, "Your father, Charlie Coffin." I carefully re-copied the message in longhand on a sheet of paper, let him sign it, and sealed it in an envelope for him.

Long after he left the office, I sat reading and re-reading the original copy. It was beautiful — the most straight-from-the-heart piece of literature I had ever seen. More than anything in the world, I wanted to tuck it away in my notebook to take back home with me and some day read to my grandchildren, or to a literature class I might be teaching. But somehow it seemed too much like prying into a private life I had no business with, so I tore it to bits and threw it in the waste basket.

Both Kopotuk and Otha are now gone and I have wished many times since that I could peek into the notebook and find the letter I destroyed.

# ARCTIC BUSH PILOT

Archie Ferguson was the most amazing character in the whole of the Arctic. Everyone knew a little about him, and a few people knew a lot. But I'm sure no one ever knew everything about this short, plump, twinkly-eyed little guy with the raspy laugh and the big grin. He was the most spectacular bush pilot that ever graced the Arctic, but actually he didn't do as much flying as many of the other pilots in the Kobuk country. It's just that he made a lot of history in a much shorter time.

Archie was a born extrovert with a big sense of humor that showed up in unexpected places. Whenever he carried a cheechako in his plane, he never missed the chance to cut out his motor unexpectedly somewhere along the way and then explain to his terrorized passenger that this always happened when you crossed the Arctic Circle. Once during the war years when he called in from the air for some high

priority information, the voice at the control tower told him such information could be given out only in case of an extreme emergency. And Archie's reply, soon to become famous among his Arctic neighbors was, "Any time I'm in the air, it's an emergency!"

Archie and his younger brother Warren were raised on their parents' gold claims on California Creek, somewhere up above Kobuk. They eventually moved to a spot between Shungnak and Kobuk, where the older Ferguson built a home for his family that was later sold to the federal government and became the CAA (Civil Aeronautics) station. Archie learned to fly while the family lived there.

"I had a helluva time learning how to set a plane down on that piece of muck up there," he told us once between cackly little laughs. "Every time my mother heard me coming, she'd stuff a stick of wood into the kitchen stove so I'd have smoke coming out the chimney to give me some wind direction. I'll never forget the time she didn't have any wood on hand so she burned up my dad's best pair of wool trousers." Then the laughing stopped and he suddenly became thoughtful. "My dad never forgot it, either,"

16

he ended in a softer tone.

Our dealings with Archie weren't always the happiest ones, but for some reason he was one man you couldn't stay mad at forever. If he got the best of you in a bargain, he always did it with a smile on his face and usually made up for it by doing you a small favor of some sort in exchange. There was a lot of prestige in being able to spin a yarn to your peers on long winter evenings about the time you made a deal with Archie and came out on the short end.

But today I think back fondly of that fascinating man and feel honored that I was fortunate enough to know him. There was a lot of good in Archie and to hold his own in the Arctic he had to stand up and fight. He did.

Once a year when the government boat, the *North Star,* came up the coast from Seattle to Barrow, it stopped at major ports along the way to unload annual supplies for all the native villages. Goods for the Selawik, Kobuk and Noatak valleys were all unloaded at Kotzebue, then sent up the various rivers by barge. Archie, for years, had held the contract to lighter goods off the ship and deliver them to their final destinations. It was a thankless job and no way on earth could anyone have done it satisfactorily. There were constant repercussions and endless complaints from unhappy teachers when cases of food were broken into or fresh fruit was frozen solid on arrival. Regardless of where the real blame should be laid, it always landed on Archie's shoulders. He accepted it gracefully and I doubt he ever lost a wink of sleep over it.

No way in the world could this busy little man personally supervise the lightering of cargo from ship to shore, storing it in his huge warehouse on the beach, then the sorting and reloading onto barges that made the journeys up the rivers.

He always chose the most capable of the group to manage the operation, but at best, the arrangement wasn't very good. With an immense amount of freight having to be handled in such a short time, the warehouse was utter confusion.

We teachers soon learned that no way in the world could a case of mixed nuts or mushrooms or mandarin oranges escape all the pitfalls along the way. Such delicacies always left Seattle, but seldom lived long enough to see the end of the journey. Our wholesale houses cooperated as best they could with us on that score. Food most vulnerable to pilferage was packed inside other boxes labelled spinach or sauerkraut.

The worst of the pilferage, I think, took place on the barges after they left Kotzebue. Archie supplied food and a cook for his men on the trips up river, and the crews assumed that part of the deal included the privileges of using up whatever stores they had on board that struck their fancy. They made no secret of the fact that they helped themselves to whatever they saw and wanted. Since a trip to the head of the Kobuk could take as much as two weeks, depending on high or low water, storms, delays in the villages or motor troubles, the Shungnak and Kobuk freight sometimes got hit rather hard.

There were other complications, too. The barges never got underway until late August or early September. By this time the fingers of winter were creeping over the tundra and rivers slowing up and lowering in depth in preparation for freeze-up. There was no way to protect the freight from freezing weather, so we seldom got our canned goods undamaged.

When you go for a year at a time without a taste of fresh bologna or wieners or a real potato or an egg with a shell on it, you can let yourself get carried away at the very thought of Archie's barge chugging around the bend. I remember the year we ordered the case of fresh celery. The barge arrived late in the afternoon when the sun had already set. Marvin was on the river bank to pick up our fresh goods as soon as it was unloaded.

Whatever else came that night I don't recall; I only remember the fateful celery. Marvin pried open a board from the top of the box just to check it out. The poor thing had gone through so many freezings and thawings that it was a mess of mush. He could put his hand straight through it from top to bottom without touching much of anything solid.

He wiped his arm off the best he could on the frozen ground, hammered the box closed again with a stone; and leaving his cargo on the river bank, he came storming up the hill in a fit of rage and disappointment.

"You should see that celery, Lou! Rotten! Rotten right to the bottom."

"Oh, no!" I wailed.

"Oh, yes! I'll just send that whole mess right back down to Archie and let him figure out what to do with it."

I agreed with him, but the more we thought about it, the more we wondered if possibly there might be a little bit of celery in the center that was salvageable.

"We know very well that Archie won't do anything about it," I rationalized. "Even if he absorbed the price of the freight up river, we'll still have to pay for the celery plus all that freight from Seattle to Kotzebue."

Our annual supplies were ordered through the Alaska Native Service and they came up on a government boat from Seattle. The cost for goods and freight was taken out of our pay checks before we ever saw them, and our office was not inclined to listen to complaints.

The colder and darker and later it got, the more we wondered about our box sitting on the river bank.

"If there is anything worth saving in that box, it won't last much longer. We aren't going to gain a thing by letting it sit there and freeze solid again. I suppose I could go down and get it."

So at ten o'clock Marvin pulled his parka off the top of the kitchen door where he always hung it, stuffed a flashlight into his pocket, and toted his celery up the hill. We spent the next two hours scooping the slimy outside layers off each bunch of celery down to the hearts that had somehow survived. We ended up with the equivalent of two or three bunches, but we nibbled it sparingly and paid our bill.

Archie's mail contract was a difficult one to fulfill. He was supposed to bring the mail up river once a month from June through September. The agreement was that he would carry it on his barge as he delivered freight, but it was apparent to everyone involved that the contract was an unrealistic one. He didn't haul freight once a month and it wasn't feasible to make the trip just for the mail. If we got two bargeloads of freight a week apart the last half of August, we also got two batches of mail. This qualified for two of the four months, but on the other two he sometimes had to default.

And, of course, everyone in the Arctic delighted in the escapades of Archie as concerned the two Caterpillar tractors he had at the head of the Shungnak River.

Some years earlier, Archie had gone to the lower states and sold stock in what was to be the Alaska-Kobuk Mining Company. He hauled in some big equipment across the tundra with huge Cats to work the mine. The mine never materialized, and two of the Cats he used for transportation never made it back to the river. They mired down somewhere along the trail where they sat for a good many years. It was Archie who finally decided the time had come to claim them as salvage and haul them out. How he got them across the tundra to the Kobuk, I'm not sure; but I believe he sent men in during the winter when the tundra was frozen and they warmed the Cats up, started the engines and drove them to the river bank on their own power. That proved to be the easiest and least spectacular part of the trip.

Archie had recently had built to his specifications a beautiful fifty thousand dollar tunnel barge with an inboard motor and a propeller inside the lower half of the structure. He used the boat first on his freighting up the Kobuk and it made history all over the Arctic. Whole villages lined up on the river bank as it pulled in to shore just to see this remarkable contrivance and how well it operated. Archie gloried in his new toy. This may have been what brought on his hairbrained idea about salvaging the Cats. The tractors were sitting on the river bank above Kiana waiting for a ride home and Archie had instructed his crew on their last trip home at the end of the freighting season to load the Cats onto the empty barge and take them in to Kotzebue.

The boys loaded the tractors like a crew of old pros and fastened them together with the biggest chain they had, but they failed to chain them to anything else. They parked them on the bed of the barge, equidistant from either side. Everything went fine until, just at the mouth of the Kobuk where the river enters Kobuk Lake, the water got a little rough. The barge began to list with the weight of water that had leaked into the bottom part; and with each listing, the Cats slipped in a little further to the low side. Finally it happened. The tractors skidded far enough to upend the barge and, still chained together, they flopped over into 20 feet of water.

It didn't take long for the news of the disaster to reach Kotzebue, and Archie flew apart into bits and pieces in every direction. He jumped into the closest airplane he could get his hands on and bombed on up to the mouth of the Kobuk. His crew that had intended to move into port without their load, heard that plane from the time it left Kotzebue and knew they'd better be doing something that looked at least businesslike before it reached them. So when Archie arrived, they had every available rope and chain dangling over the edge of the barge.

He zoomed in as low as he dared, opened his window and circled on one wingtip around and around while he yelled instructions to them as to how they should hook on to their lost tractors and haul them up again. Of course, nothing happened, and a frustrated little pilot finally tootled off back to Kotzebue with his tractors in the bottom of the Kobuk.

There were always plenty of people standing by waiting to get a stab back at Archie for past grievances and here was a chance. Someone reported him to the Coast Guard for obstructing a navigable river with dangerous machinery lodged at the bottom of the channel. Soon thereafter, he received a letter from the Coast Guard informing him that he was in violation and would have to remove his Cats from the river.

Archie was ready for them. Every winter the villagers in Kotzebue, for lack of proper garbage facilities, stored all their trash, including honey bucket waste, in oil drums at the back doors of their cabins. Drums were plentiful in those days, since all the government installations used a fantastic amount of fuel every winter and the drums weren't worth shipping back to Seattle. They were free for the taking. But come spring, something had to be done with the garbage. So just before breakup, barrels by the dozens were dog teamed out onto the ice in Kotzebue Sound in front of the village and left to disappear into the water when the ice went out.

Whether or not those drums at the bottom of the Sound ever interfered with Archie's lightering business or not is beside the point. The fact that they existed was enough. He sent a blistering message back to the Coast Guard that when the village of Kotzebue got rid of the hundreds of barrels that had accumulated in the ocean in front of the village over a period of years, he would get rid of his two tractors at the bottom of the Kobuk. So each rested his case.

# A FIGHT FOR LIFE

Although Marvin continually preached the doctrine that the white man would invade the Arctic and the Eskimos must be prepared to protect themselves against that invasion and even though many of the younger men agreed with him, it didn't happen overnight. The very character of the Arctic itself, with its unforgiving harshness, slowed this process. The invasion came but many fell by the wayside.

One of the signatures in our guest book says Al Fleener, February 11, 1947.

Al was the victim of a fever — not gold fever, but fur fever. He was a tall, gangly lad of 16 years, red headed and freckled, and with his left arm missing just below the elbow. As a child, he had been run over by a motorcycle.

Al came from California. His father, a widower, had come to Nome and married an Eskimo woman. When the price list for the fur markets came out in the fall of 1946, the big news was that marten skins had skyrocketed to three hundred seventy-five dollars apiece. This had never happened before; so everyone in Alaska, including Al Fleener's father, decided to go trapping. Al had just recently come to Alaska, so he agreed to go with his dad up to Walker Lake and set up a trapline.

Walker Lake was a controversial spot to begin with. It lay up above us about a hundred mile or so, at the head of the Kobuk River. In years past the Eskimos of the Upper

Kobuk had used it as a summer fishing grounds; but a story, handed down from a generation past, put an end to the summer migrations. A young man, so the story went, paddling around the lake in his kayak, was swallowed, kayak and all, by a giant fish. So in our time, Walker Lake was a taboo. No one went there any more.

The Fleeners had never been to the lake, but they made their decision to choose that as a trapping spot on the basis of information they got in Nome. Some man had told them he had been up there in 1939 and lived in a cabin he found. This cabin, they thought, could provide shelter for them.

The Fleeners were inexperienced woodsmen and had never been in the real Arctic. They equipped themselves with the poorest clothing one could possibly choose — army surplus parkas that had seen their best days, and worst of all, hard-soled mukluks. Hard soles are made from the skin of large seals — oogruk they call it. It's fine for tramping in wet muskeg during the summer but no good at all for cold weather. The uppers were made of sealskin but had no drawstrings to keep out the snow. In Kotzebue they got together some food supplies, traps, sleeping bags, sled, guns and a tent. Then they made arrangements with Bill (Pete) Peterson, our mail pilot, to take them to Walker Lake.

Just before Christmas Pete took the two men and their first load of gear up to their trapping grounds. He had all their supplies except their food and there was no room for that. He would return within the week and bring the second load, he said. But back in Kotzebue his plane was grounded with wind damage during a storm and by the time he got it back in the air the temperature had dropped to sixty below. It stayed right there for six weeks and Pete didn't get back to Walker Lake.

The cabin the Fleeners had depended on might have been habitable in 1939, but by 1946 all that remained was the

bottom half of the four walls. Al and his dad put up their tent inside the walls, hoping to get some protection at least from the wind. They set out a dozen traps, ate sparingly of the few rations they had brought with them, and sat it out in the tent waiting for Pete to return.

When it's 60 below, the animals hole up and don't move any more than people do, so the men had no luck with their trapline. By the time they realized that Pete wasn't coming back, their food was gone. They made short treks out from the tent hoping to find game they could shoot, but their poor footgear soon sent them back to the campfire to keep from freezing their feet.

Finally one day they hiked further than usual and met up with a small group of caribou. They shot and dressed out one of them, but by this time it was mid-afternoon and almost totally dark. Daylight was long hours away and the temperature was dropping even lower. They tried to establish some directions, and had to admit they were lost. Al was even more exhausted than his father, so the older Fleener left his son with the meat and started out in search of their camp. He found it eventually, but it was morning before he was able to get back to the caribou kill, and during the night Al had frozen his feet badly. They carried as much of the meat back to camp with them as they could manage but it did them little good. Their stomachs couldn't cope with it, and the food went through them like water.

December slipped by. January came and went but there was no let-up in the terrible cold. The two men survived on practically nothing in the line of food and finally decided to walk out. They packed their guns, tent and sleeping bags — even their traps — on to the long sled and started walking down the tributary that led into the Kobuk. Al's feet were paining him badly and his father wasn't in much better shape. He had frozen both thumbs and some toes, too. The load was more than they could haul, so shortly they threw away the traps. Little by little they discarded their guns and the tent. Al lagged worse each day and finally sleep began to dog him. His father pounded on him to keep him going, and when that did no good he loaded the boy on to the sled and pulled it.

They reached the Kobuk at last, and there they made the luckiest decision of their lives. Instead of attempting the ninety mile trip down river to Kobuk, for some reason, they

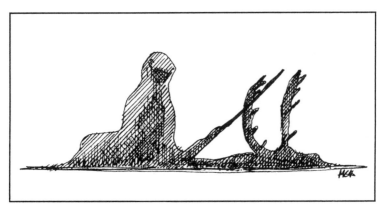

struck out straight across country to Norutak Lake about twenty five miles to the south. Here Guy Moyer had a comfortable cabin, cache and mining claims.

Guy always hitched up his team of dogs before Christmas each year and mushed down river to spend two weeks during the holidays with the people of Shungnak and Kobuk. He was a handsome and well-educated man in his thirties, a good conversationalist, and welcome in every home. Each Christmas season he would spend several evenings at our house with a pot of tea and plate of homemade cookies while he'd spin fabulous yarns about his experiences at his little kingdom on the claims. Guy was never in any hurry to leave the villages, but even if he had been, the continuous cold weather in this instance would have kept him off the long trail back. He stayed in Kobuk and Shungnak all through January and the first part of February.

He was still down river when the two Fleeners stumbled on to his cabin — as close to the end of their rope as two men could be and still keep going. They managed to break into the cabin where luckily Guy had dry kindling and firewood stacked up, and a big jar of hard Christmas candy on the table. Here they kept warm and lived on the candy and what few groceries they found in the cupboard for almost a week. Guy said afterwards that had they broken the lock on the cache, they could have eaten like kings. He had a whole winter's store of flour, oatmeal, sugar, coffee and all the food staples necessary to life in a miner's camp. But the Fleeners hadn't lived in Alaska long enough to know about the unwritten law of the land. In a case of survival, you didn't call it stealing. But they already had visions of being taken to court for housebreaking and didn't want to add an additional charge of cachebreaking.

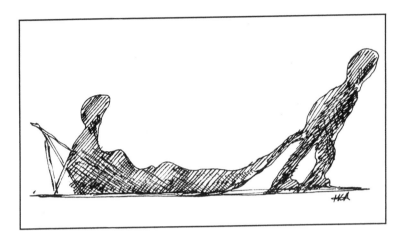

The long cold spell finally began to break. Once it was feasible to fly again, Peterson made his long-delayed trip from Kotzebue to Walker Lake. He located the empty cabin walls, followed the foot and handsled trail as far down the tributary as he could see them, and finally lost all sight of any sign of life. The men, he assumed, had frozen to death; so he flew back to Kobuk and told his story.

There was a lot of talk about starting out with dog teams to look for the missing men. But it was still bitterly cold, and ninety miles is a long trip to make with dogs. Besides, there was little hope of finding anyone alive. So the search never got beyond talk, until the story reached Dick Collins down at the CAA station.

Dick had just installed a pair of new skis on his plane and wanted to try them out. He mulled the story of the Fleeners over in his mind, wondered what he would do if he were in the same spot they were, and finally settled on the possibility of their going to Moyer's cabin. With one of his friends from the village in the back seat, he flew up the Kobuk to Norutak Lake and there he found them.

His plane was only a two-passenger craft, an army surplus L5, so the best he could do was to crowd one extra person into the back seat. Mr. Fleener insisted his son be taken out first, since he was in the poorest condition.

As luck would have it, the nurse was making her annual trip to Shungnak. Dick knew she was there, so he brought Al directly to the village. Back home, he wired Bill Peterson at Kotzebue, and the next day Bill flew to Moyer's cabin to take Al's dad into Kotzebue. We never saw the older man but we got well acquainted with his red-headed son.

Our nurse this year was a petite little lady in her early fifties, Christine Sorrill, who had come up originally from Chicago but who had spent enough years in Alaska to be a true sourdough. She always fit perfectly in every home she visited. On her annual visit, she spent a week or two in each village; and after her work was done she would take over the kitchen, much to the delight of all of us housewife-teachers who welcomed a break away from the cook stove.

Al Fleener arrived in Shungnak at a fortunate time. For the second time that day, he was in good hands. Marvin and Miss Sorrill cut away the stiff, ragged socks he had been wearing for weeks. If the socks looked bad, what was under them looked worse. All ten of his toes were black with gangrene and the smell was such as we had never experienced before. It permeated every corner of that huge building and hung there for days. With Marvin working on one foot and Miss Sorrill the other, they whittled away the worst of the black, decayed tissue, bandaged his feet, and eased a pair of big soft wool socks over the bandages.

For some reason that I still can't explain, we didn't realize at this point that the boy had been without decent food for six weeks. Instead of starting him out on soup and soft food the minute he arrived, we waited until dinner time and then feasted him on the best we could provide that evening. I had reindeer roast, rice and gravy, fresh bread and strawberry jam, powdered milk and chocolate cake. Al ate two heaping platefuls of everything, and we three so-called educated people sat right there and let him do it. In his condition, it might have killed him, but thank goodness, it didn't.

After supper, he seemed to relax and loosen up a bit. He told us something of his background and their ordeal at Walker Lake. Then he settled into the library corner and browsed through National Geographics for the rest of the evening. With the stub of his left arm holding down the pages and a six week's growth of thick curly red hair bent over his magazine, he was a sight indeed to stir the mixed emotions of all of us.

Next morning when the boy came downstairs, his eyes were almost swollen shut from crying. No doubt the shock of being transplanted so suddenly from the Walker Lake experience to the safety of a warm home with people and food had to be an emotional upset, but I am sure his shrunken stomach loaded with food had been his biggest problem that night.

Fortunately, youth has a fantastic ability to bounce back. Miss Sorrill, scheduled to go back to Kotzebue that day, was all packed long before her plane was due. So while she waited for Archie to come for her, she whipped up a big cream pie. Al pulled the kitchen stool up beside the work table and watched every move she made, then perched beside the oven waiting for the pie to bake. It was done in time for him to have a piece before he left that day. He flew out to the Kotzebue hospital with Miss Sorrill in Archie's plane and not only did he have the piece of fresh pie under his belt but I wrapped up another piece of chocolate cake for him to eat on the flight.

In the manner that all news traveled in the forties, we kept in touch with what was happening to Al Fleener. At the Native Service hospital in Kotzebue, Dr. Rabeau had to cut away most of his remaining toes. But during his stay there, Al struck up quite a friendship with the staff. He stayed on for some months and worked as handy man around the hospital. A year later Marvin saw him at a distance on one of his trips to Kotzebue, and noted that he limped quite badly. From there on, just as Pete had lost his trail up at Walker Lake, we lost his trail in Kotzebue.

## CHRISTMAS IN THE VILLAGE

Christmas season is the highlight of the year in a native village. We had our school program on Christmas Eve, and the church had one Christmas night. There were no individual Christmases, so it was a community affair. We had a big tree at school and another one in the church.

Our school building was situated at the top of a steep hill back of the village, and overlooking the river. During the winter months when the trail got icy, it was no easy matter getting up and down that hill.

The afternoon before our program, we had the school open so everyone could bring his presents, and I stayed in the classroom to help with the labeling. Most of the older people couldn't write. By late afternoon, that tree was piled up past the first circle of branches. No one wrapped gifts — just tied tags to them. They exchanged skins of all sorts, mukluks, fur "fancies" made for border trim on their parkas, and socks and gloves they had bought at the trader's store in Kobuk, ten miles up river. One fellow even gave another a string with nothing on it but a note that said, "One sheafish to be delivered after Christmas."

The whole village turned out for the program that night, even the old wrinkled bent-over ancients who probably hadn't been outside since Christmas the year before. Charlie Burbank, one of our older schoolboys, was Santa Claus. Marvin had him well padded with pillows, never realizing what would happen to them before he made his final exit. Charlie was elated over his role and bounced onto the stage on tiptoe in the manner of a ballet dancer. The school children up front began to sing softly a rhythmic Christmas song. Charlie rose to the occasion and did a few jaunty steps in time to the music. The kids, encouraged by his cooperation, raised their voices a bit, increased the tempo, and began to clap their hands in time to their chant. Charlie's feet rose higher and hit the floor harder with each step. A few of the older people began to clap and hum, first softly, then louder; and Charlie had to increase the size of the floor space he was using for his dance. Now he was bounding from one side of the stage to the other. His feet alone could no longer express the story he was trying to tell, so his hands began to take part in this fabulous exhibition.

In a matter of minutes the whole room was booming with song, hand clapping, foot stomping, and cat whistles all mixed together. Charlie's feet were spending more time in the air than on the floor. He jumped as high as he could at every beat, threw his body and hands and head around in unbelievable contortions, while he zoomed back and forth. The pillows began to shift from his chest to his belt, then slipped below his belt to his abdomen, and finally one of them sailed completely out of his shirt and landed on the stage beside him. He paid no heed — just kept cavorting, landing with one foot and then the other on the pillow that had once been his stomach, and didn't seem to notice it at all. His cap and mask bounced with every bound, went further and further askew, and finally they both tumbled off and went sailing into the audience. Charlie was wild-eyed, his face purple, and beads of perspiration from his forehead were rolling in rivulets down his cheeks. He was puffing air through his mouth; and finally, exhausted, he danced off the stage, half undressed by this time, and collapsed onto the floor behind the curtain.

Had he been in any shape for a curtain call, it would have been justified. The stomping and clapping and cheering went on and on. Then we gathered up Santa Claus's scattered costume, put him back together, and the program resumed.

The Junior Red Cross had sent us boxes of gifts for the school children, and there were sacks of candy and fruit for every person in the village. We were thankful no one had been short-changed, because Marvin and I were surrounded by gifts we hadn't expected. I received a hand-carved ivory bracelet from the lay-reader missionary's son, a purse made of two wolf heads and lined with bright red crepe from the trader's wife at Kobuk, a sik-sik (ground squirrel) skin, birch bark basket for berry picking, hand knit gloves, wolf-head mittens, and a yellow ribbon. Marvin was given a piece of jade from Jade Mountain down river, an ivory letter opener from the boy who made the bracelet, and a black bearskin rug.

The gift presentations were accompanied by jesting and laughter. So when the bearskin was pulled from the tree branches and handed to Marvin, the crown cheered and clapped.

Marvin pulled his eyebrows together and pretended bewilderment.

"What do I do with it?" he asked, addressing his question to the whole room.

"Use it like a sled!" someone shouted. "Sit on it and slide down hill!"

Laughter again, but the skin did make a wonderful sled to go scooting on down to the village. When it needed cleaning, I simply turned it upside down with the fur against the snow, and did my sliding that way.

I had arranged for one of the village girls to make me a beautiful pair of beaded calfskin slippers with hard oogruk bottoms for Marvin's Christmas present, and had them hanging on the school tree for everyone to admire. Unfortunately, he put them on and wore them for the rest of the evening. As soon as the schoolroom cleared out and we returned to our own living quarters in the back part of the building, he started into the basement to check the light plant. But he got there sooner than he expected. Those slippery oogruk bottoms hit the top step and that was all. In one nonstop hurdle that would have rivaled Santa Claus's capers that evening, he cleared ten steps and landed on the basement floor.

· · · · · · ·

So much for the white man's Christmas. The school was our domain. We imposed our customs on the children and they went along with it gracefully. But the Friend's Church down in the village was in their world. So Christmas night they did it their way and it was our turn to conform.

The Collinses, a young couple who lived in and operated the weather station three miles up river from us, mushed their dogs down to the village Christmas day to eat reindeer steak dinner with us and go to the church program. We were still sitting at the table when Dick suddenly looked at his watch and exclaimed, "Do you realize that program is starting right now!"

We bounced off our chairs and began scrambling for parkas and mitts.

"Do you suppose they'll start it without us?" we girls wondered.

But there was no need to worry. The church was packed and everyone was waiting for us. A front-row bench had been reserved, and three ushers escorted us. The village chief was master of ceremonies.

"Welcome, Mr. and Mrs. Warbelow and Mr. and Mrs. Collins," he greeted us. "Come right up here and sit down. The boys have some seats for you."

Chief led the prayer, announced each number as it was presented, and passed out gifts with the help of three or four young fellows he called from the congregation. Everyone, from children to old people, took part in the program. The children did almost all their numbers in English and then in Eskimo. The oldsters, with a maximum of delay and confusion in each case, went to the stage in groups to sing. The delay didn't bother the audience. No one was in a hurry to bring the evening's festivities to a close.

At one point, Chief dangled three strings from the ceiling and tied a muffin to the end of each at face level. The corners of his mouth twitched despite his attempts to look severe. "You, Jim, come up here!"

A teen-age boy scrambled to the stage.

"And you, Frank — George — come up!" Chief indicated each boy with a jerk of his head, and two more lads jumped on stage beside Jim, eyes twinkling with excitement.

The chief tied each boy's hands behind his back with a big handkerchief. Then with a child positioned behind each muffin, he gave the command "Go!" and the contestants raced to see who could eat his muffin first.

The older people had evidently never learned to sit on benches for any length of time, because there was a space on the floor for them to sit up front, close to the stage. I recalled one night earlier at a school meeting when the oldsters started getting tired, they slid from their benches to the floor and slept.

Their tree decorating customs were quite different from ours. The tree had been too tall for the room. But while we would have shortened it from the bottom, they cut it off at the top. The blunt top that remained pressed tightly against the ceiling, forming a soft green ring against the logs. It was decorated with rolls of crepe paper, carefully rolled and saved from previous Christmases. I felt a sharp pang of homesickness when I recalled how we did the same thing in the little country school I grew up in back in Wisconsin.

Just as our tree up at school had been the night before, the tree at church was stacked with gifts; and the branches were loaded with small things such as gloves, socks, and miniature dolls. Each gift had a lengthy card attached. The ushers distributed gifts one at a time, and each waited his turn so the notes on the cards could be read aloud. Most of this activity was in Eskimo, each note being followed by laughter and much hilarity. If the note was a special prize, the usher would read it a second time in English so we four visitors could have a chance to laugh, too.

． ． ． ． ． ．

Christmas night at church was only the beginning of their gift exchanging. The next night they went back again. This time people had a chance to give gifts to those who had given to them the evening before. So it went for several nights, each gathering having a smaller turnout, until they gave up and announced it officially ended. Gifts that were received Christmas night often showed up on the tree the next night as a gift to a third person, and that person in turn could pass it on if he wished. One of the men told Marvin that he started out giving a package of cigarettes and ended up with a nice pair of leather gloves.

While the gift giving was gradually wearing itself out those evenings between Christmas and New Years, we spent the days having games and races on the river ice. There were dog races and snowshoe races, but the ball games were the wildest of all. Every afternoon the whole village congregated on the river for a game they called football. Their ball was made of reindeer hide stuffed with reindeer hair and shaped

41

like an oversized baseball. If there were any rules, we never figured them out. The game started with someone's kicking the ball, and from then until the end it was every man for himself. They rolled, tumbled, and jumped on top of one another in one big monkey pile with the ball at the bottom. Whenever the ball slipped out from under it all and either rolled or was kicked clear of the tangled heap of bodies, the race started all over again.

The basketball games were no better. Some teacher before us had unwittingly mounted baskets at each end of Marvin's classroom, and we just as unwittingly had failed to take them down. We had to clear all the furniture from his room — it doubled as a gym. Their basketball didn't have any more rules than the football did. They usually played men against the women. Once the referee tossed the ball for the two centers, he ducked his head, ran for his life, and wasn't heard from again. The game went on nonstop with no holds barred, until the teams were too tired and mutilated to go any further. Marvin got dragged into playing a game one night, and it cured him forever. He came out of that ordeal with fingernail gouges all over him and his new Pendleton shirt ripped to pieces.

Those holidays in the middle of a long, bleak winter were some of the happiest times of the year for us. But the ball games and races, like the revolving gift giving, finally died out. Little by little the village settled back to normal. It was a Christmas season we didn't forget.